GOING HOME

THE ENTREPRENEURS GUIDE TO COPING WITH THE FAMILY

This e-book has been written for informational entertainment purposes only. Every effort has been made to make this ebook as complete and accurate as possible. However, there may be mistakes in typography or content. This ebook should be used as a guide - not as the ultimate source - as the author has written from personal experiences not professional expertise.

The purpose of this ebook is to educate and entertain. The author and the publisher do not warrant that the information contained in this e-book is fully complete and shall not be responsible for any errors or omissions. The author and publisher shall have neither liability nor responsibility to any person or entity with respect to any loss or damage caused or alleged to be caused directly or indirectly by this ebook.

Should the reader find themselves in any situation that could result in harm coming to any of the parties involved, please seek emergency or professional assistance immediately!!

Why We Wrote This Book

Why We Wrote This Book

After joyously supporting ourselves for the last couple of decades through our online businesses, our families still have no idea what we do. Seriously. We have tried to explain over and over, but somehow it just never quite sinks in.

We still show up at family events and are greeted with snarky comments like "Really? I would have thought you would have gotten tired of that by now." or the lovely "I bought an ebook a while back. Total rip-off. Was that yours?".

Now maybe your family is better, or at least different, than ours, but the bottom line is that they were not supportive when we were kids, and they haven't changed since then. Well, actually that is not true, they have gotten worse as we have become more successful.

So this book is for every entrepreneur that dreads going home for the holidays or any other time. It is for every internet marketer that is tired of suffering through another snipe at the hands of a toxic parent, and needs the tools to get past the guilt, and move on towards a happy life.

Ultimately, how you deal with your own family issues is up to you. You may decide to tough it out and stay connected by preparing yourself better for the visits, or you may decide that going the 'no contact' route is the best path to self-preservation. No matter what your decision, we hope this helps a bit along the way.

Understanding The Problem

"Families are messy. Immortal families are eternally messy.
Sometimes the best we can do is to remind each other that
we 're related for better or for worse... and try to keep the
maiming and killing to a minimum. "
~Rick Riordan

Understanding the Problem

First of all, understand that you are not the only grown adult that melts into a quivering mass of jelly at the thought of heading home for a visit. If you live far away, and don't see the family often, there is a good chance that there is a

reason why you live on the far side of the continent from them.

Bumpy family relationships are not uncommon, but entrepreneurs seem to have more than most, in large part because we have chosen paths so very different form our parents.

Unfortunately, very few of them actually have a firm grasp on what we do, sometimes because they simply don't understand the technology of the world that we live in, and sometimes simply because, well, they don't really want to.

And sometimes the chasm is much deeper than simply not understanding what we do: we represent the dreams they never pursued and the risks they never took. Where some parents point to their self-employed offspring with pride, to others we are a daily reminder of the things they did not do, the paths that were too risky for them to venture down. In other words, some will see us as the light shining on their own self-perceived failures, no matter how successful we may see them.

There are also families that fall into much more serious categories, those that can be classified only as toxic, that are emotionally or physically abusive, or both. Both can leave scars that follow us well into adulthood, and only you can decide if they are worth the risk of continued involvement or going total dark 'no contact'.

It's sometimes difficult to know which category your own family falls into, but to be honest, it doesn't always matter because the end result is the same: going home for the holidays or a family event is a miserable and often traumatic event, that drains your energy and your spirit for weeks, both before and after.

And if you are an entrepreneur, this can have a serious long-term effect on your productivity and creativity, which is definitely going to have a negative impact on your business and your income, not to mention your emotional and physical well-being.

As entrepreneurs, we are often little 'stand alone' business centers, and the sole responsibility of motivation and progress rests entirely on our own shoulders. We don't have the crowd at the water cooler to pump us up after a bad day or the Monday morning sales meeting to get the blood pumping before we hit the phones to drum up business.

Sorry, bunkie, but it is just the three of us here: Me, myself and I. That means that we cannot afford to take the time out of our lives to stress out over the trip home, whether it is one night or a whole week, we have to stand up and do the right thing...and that right thing SHOULD be thing that is right for US....not the rest of the family.

And that is where this is about to get really bumpy, because one of the big decisions you need to make is whether spending the holidays with The Family is really The Right Thing *or not.*

And - just to complicate matters even more - you night want to take a look at what drove you to become an entrepreneur in the first place:

- Did you resent being told what to do by your boss?

- Did you find yourself working longer hours than anyone else to please the boss anyway?

- Did you get angry with yourself for being so happy for any scrap of approval thrown your way?

We could go on, but you may be seeing a pattern here....many of us stepped away from the corporate world simply because it was too reminiscent of our childhoods. The more controlling one or both parents were, the more we chafe against 'authority'. The less positive re-enforcement we received at home, the more we crave it through our jobs.

Unfortunately, as most of us discovered once we hit the working world - very few jobs provide much in the way of daily kudos.

Consequently, many of us have chosen to become our own boss, and therefore have more control over our work environment, which is more than a bit ironic

CHAPTER: 3

when you consider that our upbringing may well be responsible for the career path we

chose and that they now disapprove of.

To Go Or Not To Go

That truly is the damned question

~ apologies to W. Shakespeare

To Go Or Not To Go

That truly is the biggest question. There are times when going home is definitely optional: holidays, birthdays, Ground Hog Day, the christening of your second cousin's 7th kid. Depending on the event (Christmas versus christening, for example), the fallout of non-attendance may be loud, but probably won't get you kicked off the A-list for next time.

But there are also times when staying away will cause monumental repercussions, such as being absent for a parent's final days, funerals, and weddings. Think long and hard about the long term effects before you decide you truly need to avoid these occasions.

And you need to fully understand what those long-term effects really are, beyond the possibility of getting cut out of the will or wholesale shunning by the rest of your relatives.

You truly need to consider how you will feel a year from now if you don't go home. Can you handle that you were not there when your father died - or was the relationship so bad that you can handle not being there easier than being present, and facing his possible last hurtful words? To be honest, there is no good or easy answer to some questions. No matter which path you take, there will be consequences, and only you can honestly answer the question. Whatever you do, though, don't rush the decision. If the situation allows, take the time to think things through thoroughly, and make a well-thought out choice, carefully balancing the pros & cons.

These are the types of decisions where you don't get a do-over. The likelihood is that neither decision, going or not going, will be 100% right - but one will be better than the other, the proverbial 'lesser of two evils' and that may be as good as your options will ever get.

Still, even when faced with the long-term and potentially serious aftermath, there may be extremely valid reasons for staying away: if you have suffered any kind of serious abuse, physical or mental, at the hands of someone that will also be attendance, you have every right, no, *you have an obligation to yourself,* to put yourself first, and stay away.

If you have been physically abused, in any way, by anyone that will be in attendance at a family function, don't go. It is that simple. Family obligation does not outweigh the obligation to yourself.

Emotional abuse, is a different animal altogether. You may never have been on the wrong end of your Dad's belt - but the constant little verbal jabs ('You just don't have a knack for sports, do you?', 'No more after school snacks for you, you're getting pudgy') from our parents do as much if not more damage to our psyche (think long term adult selves) than we realize.

Until. We. Are. Adults. And dealing with the issues from our childhood.

You may not have a plaster cast on your spirit, but the shadows left by the daily snipes of a toxic parent can haunt you forever. As mentioned previously, many of us actually left the corporate world because working for a boss was eerily 'eminiscent of being home with the parents again, and that just took all the fun out of that

weekly paycheck.

Think about that for a moment - why did you REALLY hate working for someone else? I hated

it because I spent my childhood trying to get my mother's approval, and found myself working

stupid long hours at every job trying to get my boss's approval too.

Guess what? That worked out about the same as it did with Mom, but at least I did get paid for

the pain and suffering at my job.

But I digress.

If you have been abused, emotionally or physically, you are dealing with more than just the

'normal' stress of dealing with family, you are dealing with a truly toxic family situation.

Going home brings you within their circle of influence again, and undoes all that .vonderful

self-confidence that you have spent years building up, and possibly orse.

Only you can decide if the fall-out of not going home outweighs the effects of being with your

family. If you spend weeks dreading the upcoming visit, and a week curled up in a fetal ball,

binge watching the Hallmark channeldo you

really need to go home?

Take this quick quiz to help you decide:

1) Who will be the most angry if you do not attend this event?

____

____

____

____

2) How do you feel about this person's
response?____

____

____

____
____

3) What do you fear will happen if you do not
attend?____

____

____

____
____

4) What do you fear will happen if you do attend?

____

____

____

____

5) How long will this person's anger be likely to last if you do not
attend?____

____

____

____
____

6) How long will attending this event affect you - before AND after the
event?____

____

____

____
____

Take a moment to reflect on your answers above. Which is going to have the greatest long term affect on your life: going home or staying home?

Whatever the decision you make, remember this: it's your life, and you do have the right to make the decision that is best for you. That is not selfish, that is self-care.

Family: Friend or Foe

Absence makes the heart grow fonder.

~ Anonymous

<u>Family: Friend or Foe</u>

Very often, when we have been away from the family for a while, we tend to look back at the past through a warm hazy glow that softens reality, a reality that usually hits like a sledge hammer, sometimes within minutes of getting off that plane:

Mom: "Wow, don't worry about those extra pounds you've put on, I can get you into my killer bootcamp class. You'll lose 10 pounds before you head home. No one will recognize you."

Dad: "Why did you bring your laptop along? Can't you stay off Facebook for a couple of days?"

Uncle Tom: "Nobody actually buys anything online unless you count Amazon. It's too dangerous. So what do you REALLY do?"

Depending on your history with your family, you know before you arrive that the comments will probably range from the mildly annoying to full- blown toxicity, depending on the person you are interacting with.

As much as you would like to head home to the picture perfect rendition of "Home for the Holidays", you know it's more likely to be the Titanic revisited, with everyone clawing over the drowning victims to save themselves.

You should also face facts and understand that the perfect family is a myth created by the greeting card companies, and the therapy industry. Every family has it's own level of crazy, whether it is an Aunt Hazel who starts singing Christmas carols on the front porch, wearing only a lamp shade, or Cousin Bobby who shows up at every family event hawking his latest Ponzi scheme, or the sister that arrives with a new husband for every major holiday.

They may be tiring to annoying or even occasionally embarrassing, but they are not truly damaging most of the time (unless you are trying to match Aunt Hazel sherry for sherry, then your liver may be in jeopardy).

Unfortunately, that is not always the case. Sadly, there may also be some truly toxic relatives hanging on your family Christmas tree, and those are the ones you need to prepare for because here is one important fact you need to remember and hold close: You are not going to change them.

You can, however, change the way you react to them.

The first step in surviving the holidays with the family, is to look more closely at the areas that are causing the pain points for you. Take an honest look at which family members you are dreading interaction with the most, and then drill down to why.

The whys are often the most difficult to ascertain. On the surface level, it may be that you feel your Dad questions you too much about your career choice because he disapproves, but take a deeper look at how you react to the questions and you may find that it bothers you because you have the same concerns.

Then again - it may also be because he has never been supportive of anything that you have done, and you deeply resent his taking the same tact regarding your entrepreneurial career. Looking at how Dad dealt with your personal decisions as you were growing up will give you a great deal of insight into where he is coming from today - and whether he is 'friend or foe' today.

Here are some questions that can help you prepare for the visit home:

7) Who are the people that you dread seeing the most?

____

____

____

____

____

8) What is the key point of friction between you? (for each person listed above)

____

____

____

____

9) What are typical comments from each

person?____

____

____

____

____

10) What is your usual response to each person?

____

____

____

____

The Strategy: Disarm & Diffuse

"Every battle is won or lost before it's ever fought" ~ **Sun Tzu** *"The Art of War"*

The Strategy: Disarm & Diffuse

As mentioned in the last chapter, you are probably not going to change your family members and how they behave, but you can change how you react by planning ahead for the expected trauma.

Sometimes it helps to simply pretend you are in a sitcom, okay, it's a really bad sitcom, but you get the idea.

When Aunt Hazel hits the sherry and starts rocking out on the front porch, you can either join in, or just sit back with your own glass and chuckle at the crazy antics of the octogenarian (what? you didn't know Aunt Hazel was that old?). And do remember that you may be the next generation's 'Aunt Hazel', so maybe you can cut her some slack.

Aunt Hazel and her caroling issues aside, not all of the family issues are resolved this easily. We wish. The truth is that you probably have a very good reason for dreading the trip home, and making light of it, or worse

yet, ignoring it, is not going to make it go away.

So let's take a look at the answers to the 'pop quiz' in the last chapter, and see what we can do to defuse these possible flareups before they happen:

Question 1: Who are the people that you dread seeing the most?

This is a very important question - is it really the whole family that you want to avoid or is just your Aunt Hazel? Dad? Your Sister?

Determining the 'who' will help you map out the best way to avoid or deal with the situation.

Question 2: What is the key point of friction between you?

How bad is the friction? On a scale of 1 to 10, with 1 being soothed with a piece of your hidden chocolate stash and 10 being time to look up the phone number for the local bail bondsman, where do things <u>really</u> fall? All kidding aside, you need to truly come to an honest assessment of just how serious an impact the time with family will have on your life and your lifestyle.

There is a huge difference between being annoyed for 3 days and putting yourself back into a truly toxic environment. Now is the time to decide where your family situation really ranks.

Question 3: What are typical comments from each person?

Is Aunt Hazel really just nosey? Is Cousin Bobby just an idiot who drives you nuts with his incessant schemes and stupid questions? Are Dad's comments really thinly veiled demands that you give up your dreams and follow in his footsteps, with very real consequences if don't go along?

Question 4: What is your usual response to each person?

This is critical - identifying the hot points that you have with each person that has you in melt-down mode right now, and how you normally respond. Look at this list carefully, and remember back to the last few interactions that you had with each person.

Was it an appropriate response or was it a build-up of past frustrations and unvoiced anger?

An eruption that may have been larger than the current situation actually merited?

Now that you have identified the person/s and actions or events that are setting off your personal alarm bells, it's time to see what we can do to a) avert the situation or b) diffuse the situation.

In either case, our goal is to minimize the impact of these potential situations and still let you enjoy (more or less) being home with the family.

11) How can you minimize your time or activities with the person/persons from #1?

____

____

____

____

12) Who can you reach out to that may be able to help with each person?____

____

____

____

____

13) How would you *like* to respond to each person this time?____

____

____

____

______

14) Write down a response to each typical comment from Question 3 that will make you feel better about the interaction while still diffusing the situation:

____

____

____

____

____

____

____

____

____

____

____

____

____

CHAPTER: 6

Creating Your Plan of (Non) Attack

Creating Your Plan of (Non) Attack

Most of us that are self-employed are very good at planning our work flow, and maximizing our time. We see the opportunities that others miss, and pride ourselves on finding creative solutions to the most difficult problems in our business.

So why do we not apply these skills to dealing with family members? It's simple: we have been conditioned from childhood that family is just that, family. You are supposed to love them because they are family. Blood is thicker than water. blah. blah. blah.

Not true, my friends. I am willing to bet you would never allow a client or a friend to say the things to you that you have been allowing your family to say. You have a right to be treated with respect, and talked to as though you are a valued member of the family. It is your birthright as a human being.

And this is where the planning comes into play. In the previous chapter you wrote down the responses that you would LIKE to make to your relative's unwelcome comments, as well as the responses that you SHOULD make to prevent Armageddon from breaking out at your parents 50th anniversary party.

The key is that there is a huge difference between what your automatic emotional reflex response is, and the response that you would make after thinking about it for a few minutes.

After a few deep breaths, and maybe a few kicks at the garbage can, the calmer, saner side of your brain prevails, and you formulate a rational response.

What we want to prevent, with a bit of advance preparation, is that knee-jerk visceral response to your Dad's comments about your business venture, and simply prevent his comments from getting under your skin again.

And yes, you really can do that, or at least lessen the explosion.

Here's your next exercise:

15) Reach out to the person or persons listed in Question 6, and ask for their help in minimizing your interaction with the person you most wish to avoid. If the person will be at the event, set up a signal so the other person will know when to interrupt the dialogue and rescue you, or perhaps you can arrange for a friend or non-attending family member to call or text you from time to time, to provide a possible 'emergency' escape…just like you used to do on blind dates or your neighbor's annual and boring cocktail party….make sure that they understand the importance of following through for you! 16) This is the really important one: remember the well-thought out responses from Question 8? Now you are going to put them to good use - it's curtain time, folks! Put yourself in those gruesome, nasty situations with your narcissistic mother harping at you about your weight or your over-achiever- hyper-critical Dad and rehearse those carefully crafted responses.

Yes. In front of the mirror. Rehearse. Again. And again.

The key is that there is a huge difference between what your automatic emotional reflex response is, and the response that you would make after thinking about it for a few minutes.

After a few deep breaths, and maybe a few kicks at the garbage can, the calmer, saner side of your brain prevails, and you formulate a rational response.

What we want to prevent, with a bit of advance preparation, is that knee-jerk visceral response to your Dad's comments about your business venture, and simply prevent his comments from getting under your skin again.

And yes, you really can do that, or at least lessen the explosion.

Here's your next exercise:

15) Reach out to the person or persons listed in Question 6, and ask for their help in minimizing your interaction with the person you most wish to avoid. If the person will be at the event, set up a signal so the other person will know when to interrupt the dialogue and rescue you, or perhaps you can arrange for a friend or non-attending family member to call or text you from time to time, to provide a possible 'emergency' escape…just like you used to do on blind dates or your neighbor's annual and boring cocktail party….make sure that they understand the importance of following through for you! 16) This is the really important one: remember the well-thought out responses from Question 8? Now you are going to put them to good use - it's curtain time, folks! Put yourself in those gruesome, nasty situations with your narcissistic mother harping at you about your weight or your over-achiever- hyper-critical Dad and rehearse those carefully crafted responses.

Yes. In front of the mirror. Rehearse. Again. And again.

Until the words flow smoothly and flawlessly. Try variations of the responses, but you know that the attacks are usually pretty much along the same theme, so you probably won't have to get too creative with your responses. Just keep practicing until you feel your confidence come back, and your successful entrepreneurial self can be heard in the words.

There's an odd thing that often happens when you respond from a place of strength to the bullies - because that is what they are, relatives or not - they don't know what to do or how to respond because they feed on emotion, not calm logic. It baffles them, and they will very often retreat because they do not handle the unexpected very well.

You know what we call that? A big fat victory.

Chapter 7:
Plan Your Exit Before You Arrive

When given the choice between making your exit or making a scene, take the nearest exit. Please.

Plan Your Exit Before You Arrive

One of the worst aspects of visiting family is feeling trapped. Entrepreneurs are often very solitary creatures by nature; we are used to working alone, without supervision, often spending long hours in our own company, something that is apparently quite an alien concept to many people.

Consequently, spending a week closely confined with our family can be challenging - even when things are going well. I've found over the years that knowing that I can leave at any time makes it easier to cope. It's kind of like taking your umbrella along on a cloudy day - you probably won't actually need it, but you feel better knowing you have it along.

Here's some tips to help you plan: 1) Plan a couple of breaks from the family. Visit the mall to finish your holiday shopping or to pick up the clean underwear you forgot to pack. Lunch with an old friend. Check the local book stores for author events….you get the drift. Anything to get away solo for a couple of hours to refresh your soul and your attitude.

2) Don't rely on someone else for transportation. Drive home if you can, but even if you fly in, rent a car. Use the excuse that you don't want to inconvenience anyone by picking you up or you want to get together with old friends while in town. If things get really bad, and you need to make a fast exit to a local motel, grabbing the keys and leaving is a lot easier than waiting for a cab. At the very least, make sure you have the number of the local cab service on your mobile phone's favorite list or your handy Uber app. And always keep some cash tucked away in case the cab won't accept your credit card.

3) Before arriving home, reach out to a friend in town, and see if they can let you crash on their couch if the situation gets too bad.

Chances are you have friends that know the situation with your family and they will be more than happy to provide a safe haven until you can get out of town and back to the safety of your own nest.

4) My personal favorite: A few years ago, I started booking a room at a hotel about 20 minutes from my parents home. Close enough to not be too much of a commute for me, but far enough that they think twice about popping in on me unannounced. I freely admit that it went over like a lead balloon the first time, but I told them that I needed high speed internet access, which they do not have, to keep tabs on my business. It's now accepted with fairly minimal grumbling.

You may have clients in far flung countries that contact you in the wee hours of the morning, or you have a current project that you need to work on and don't   want to bother anyone with your late night hours - whatever the excuse,   staying at hotel and limiting actual contact with the family can be a life   saver.

It is definitely worth the extra expense and effort. The cost of the room? $89.73. The cost of your sanity? Priceless.

Yes, this may cause some grumbling but if you explain it correctly, your family can flip this around to fit their own narrative, allowing them to tell everyone that you are working too hard, and make it sound like they are proud of you, instead of ticked off, which of course, they are. It also makes your exit after dinner soooo much easier, and much less hostile.

The nice part about staying at the hotel is that also gives you some breathing space, and really does make the rest of the time easier to endure. Throw in a nice massage or spa treatment and things suddenly seem a lot more positive. Or go work out the frustrations at the hotel gym or the room's mini-bar. Your call. Either way, much easier to deal with that toady Cousin Ralph.

5) Use that tried and true salvation of the blind date: Have a friend call at a pre-arranged time, to give you a possible out. Sometimes a simple 'conversation interruptus' is enough to halt the progress from mild irritation to a full-blown argument. Have a good and trusted friend - preferably one the family does not know, and so will not recognize the number on your caller ID - call to see how things are going. You can then determine the next course of action based on your current situation.

CHAPTER: 8

Parameters

<u>Parameters</u>

Although your parents may make your life miserable on a regular basis about your career choice (or what they consider the lack thereof), when a family emergency arises, and you are the only one able to come home and take care of Mom and Dad, you will see an odd thing happen:

They are suddenly proud of you, telling all that will listen, that you own your own business, and can therefore come home and be there when needed.

As. Soon. As. They.

Call.

Yikes.

Yep, you can no doubt see the danger here. It is so easy to fall back into the trap of wanting to please our parents, that we willingly slide back into the same space we fought so hard to escape from. I am not advocating ignoring a genuine situation where your help is needed, but you do need to be cautious, and separate the real issue at hand from your desire to please them.

As entrepreneurs, especially if you work online, we are blessed with a certain amount of mobility and flexibility. However, contrary to what many IM books would have you believe - most of us cannot leave our businesses completely unattended for weeks on end.

And unlike your brother, the family's 'Golden Child', with the corner office, the home in the burbs, and the 2.5 children, we don't have 3 weeks of paid vacation coming up, so time off for us may mean time off from income at a certain point.

The problem is that once you answer the call to head home the *first* time, you are very likely going to be the default caregiver from that point on, and it's likely that no one else is going to step up and volunteer.

After all, it's inconvenient and maybe costly, and hey! You're self-employe, right?

And that means that you have no boss, and no one to answer to, right?

WRONG!

The is where you need to take a firm stand, and let everyone know that as much as you want to help out, you cannot go solo. Everyone needs to pitch in and help out, because you DO have a boss, and he/she is the hardest taskmaster that you have ever worked for: You.

There are times when you simply have to draw the line in the sand, and since these are people that you have probably been clashing with since childhood, this will not be easy.

But you are talking about your livelihood and your life here, so standing up and pushing back

is vital to your survival.

Amazingly, once you make it clear that you are not going to be on call 24/7/365, you may be

quite surprised to see that other family members are suddenly available to take up the slack -

or the emergency may not be quite as dire as originally portrayed.

One caveat, though: be prepared for the guilt trip if you announce you are not available to

come home to 'help out' this time. But in the name of self- preservation, take the path that is

right for you, and your future. Being the 'designated caregiver', especially for people that you

may not really like, and who may not have shown you much care in your life, is a daunting,

exhausting and thankless task.

If at all possible, don't get sucked into the drama, unless the emergency is real and your

attendance is warranted. And that is a decision that only you can make.

CHAPTER: 9

Going 'No Contact'

The next step when you realize toxic means…toxic.

<u>Going 'No Contact'</u>

For most people, this is a gut-wrenching decision, not to be entered into lightly. It usually comes after years of trying to 'repair' the relationships with our parents or siblings, and feeling guilty that you are not able to have a hallmark-card relationship with your relatives, since obviously the rest of the world adores them.

Obviously.

News flash: there is a really good chance that this mess is not all about you.

A good friend's mother screamed at her one day, during one of their epic phone battles: 'You and I have not gotten along since you were 9 years old!' and then proceeded to slam the phone down, beginning a contact-free period of 3 blissfully quiet years for my friend.

Ah, the wonderful years of still having a landline. Forcefully hitting the button on your iPhone just does not have the same effect.

My friend had felt guilt for years over her relationship with her mother, since all of her friends went shopping and had lunch with their moms on a regular basis, while convos with her mom tended to end with her in tears, and often resulted in years of dead-zone silence.

But her mother's angry proclamation caused that proverbial light to go off: who was in control of the relationship when she was 9 years old? It certainly was not the child!

And that simple comment changed forever the dynamics of their relationship, because once she understood that the 'problem' was not her, it was her mother, she was able to release the guilt that she had felt for so long and move on with her life. The relationship with her mother had been toxic all her life, and had affected every aspect of her life from her work to her personal relationships.

Instead of agonizing over every period of silence, she now relishes the peace and tranquility that her mother's absence brings. They do communicate but she keeps a tight handle on things, and lets her mother know when she is crossing the line again. The blow-ups do still occur, but she now controls her reaction to them and does not let the guilt take over her life as she once did.

How do you recognize the difference between a seriously irritating relative and a truly toxic one? Sometimes it is easy: the father that wields the belt, the brother that bullies and belittles constantly, or the mother that makes the child weight conscious at the age of 4.

But just as often, the comments are insidious, wrapped in loving platitudes that steal your self esteem away bit by bit as you are growing up. Perhaps no one in the family was allowed to voice their own opinion, or you were never encouraged to talk about school or your sports activities at mealtimes, the implication being that they were not important enough to warrant time at the dinner table.

There are a thousand ways that parents rob children of their sense of self-worth, while re-enforcing their own egos, but unfortunately, it often takes the distance of both years and miles for us to realize the damage that our 'well-meaning' parents inflicted on our psyches.

In terms of emotional abuse, the narcissistic parent is undoubtedly the best documented, and the most difficult to recover from. The dangerous part is that most of them seem perfectly normal to the rest of the world, reserving their special brand of hell for their family.

According to the Mayo Clinic, narcissistic personality disorder is defined as "a mental disorder in which people have an inflated sense of their own importance, a deep need for admiration and a lack of empathy for others. But behind this mask of ultraconfidence lies a fragile self-esteem that's vulnerable to the slightest criticism."

Narcissists don't change simply because they have children. Children are seen as possessions, tools to further their own goals, and props to boost their egos and public personas. Narcissists do not respect other's boundaries, physically or emotionally, and will often unload their emotional baggage and inappropriate personal stories onto their children. Narcissistic mothers will share their marital woes with their young daughters, while the narcissistic father may brag of his indiscretions to his young sons, making them a party to infidelity.

The problem is that we, as children, do not know what a narcissist is!

We only know that we want our parents' love and approval and so most of us do everything possible to be the 'perfect child' that our parents want.

We became 'over-achievers' in school and sports, usually baffled as to why the winning home run or the straight-A report card was never as well received as we had hoped. But deep in our hearts, we always knew that *next time, we would get it right*.

Needless to say - next time never happened. It was impossible to be quite what our parents wanted/expected/needed. The harder we tried, the more distant and unobtainable their love and approval seemed to be.

And still we tried.

Many of us were constantly in trouble at home, but we never knew quite what it was that we did wrong. The infractions were just esoteric enough that we were never quite able to pinpoint exactly where we veered off course, such things as using 'the wrong tone of voice' or one that was 'disrespectful'.

And still we tried.

And of course, the punishment would coincide with the upcoming prom or a special event that you had been looking forward to for weeks. While all your friends were off enjoying the big dance, you were home in your room.

As you grew up, you found it easier to simply agree, rather than have an opinion of your own, letting your narcissistic parent control your life more and more, just to keep the peace.

And still…..we tried.

As the child of a narcissist becomes an adult, the narcissistic parent becomes even more threatened, and their response to your growing independence and adulthood can truly turn ugly.

Unlike a normal parent who wants to raise a strong and independent adult, ready and willing to find their place in the world, narcissistic parents see their children's growing independence as a direct threat to their own little kingdom. They need to maintain control over their (reluctant) audience, something that is difficult to accomplish if their child is out of their immediate sphere of influence.

For the narcissist, a child going away to school or getting engaged becomes a full blown crises.

Where the normal parent wants their child to choose a career or life path that will make him or her happy, the narcissistic parent wants the child to follow in his or her footsteps, thereby validating the parent's life choices. To do otherwise, from the viewpoint of the narcissistic parent, is to embarrass the parent by telling the world that their child places no value on the parent's career path or life choices.

Even if Dad is self-employed, he will threaten to cut you out of the will if you start you own company, rather than go to work in the family business.

The narcissistic mother will never forgive the daughter that loves being in business, but has no desire to be a stay at home mom.

Narcissists will try to deliberately sabotage their child's sense of self-worth, and virtually destroy their self-confidence.

It's child abuse, pure and simple, but it doesn't leave an externally visible mark so the neighbors can call Child Protective Services.

If only.

As children, all we know is that home is not a happy place for us. We always felt as though we were walking on eggshells, the slightest wrong voice intonation and we would be grounded for the week. School was often the haven, and coming home the unknown: you never knew if you would be greeted with fresh-baked cookies or sent to your room.

But as an adult, among other adults, we begin to realize that not every home was like ours (although a scary number of them are). Slowly, we began to realize that our home life was not the norm, and that there are parents that are indeed involved, engaged and supportive of their offspring's endeavors.

It's one of the big wow moments in life for many of us.

And then begins the real battle - developing that sense of self-worth and value that we were denied as kids. But it happens, not without work, but it is possible with the help of good friends, and sometimes a lot of expensive therapy.

The problem is that is easy to backslide, as long as we maintain contact with the family members that have cause the issues. Our childhood 'training' is tough to overcome, and we still have a natural desire for our family's approval.

Many adult children find that the only way to have some semblance of a normal life is to sever the relationship completely, and take themselves completely out of the toxic relatives' sphere of influence.

This sounds drastic, and it is. Even when you know that this is the very best decision that you can make for your own sake - that does not make it an easy one.

Very often the initial decision is made in the heat of the moment, during an argument or heated phone call, and the guilt and second thoughts start creeping on over the ensuing weeks or months, most likely with calls or visits from other family members. Some may support your decision but others may not.

Additionally, the family member that you are trying to expel from your life will probably make a very concerted effort to deflect the blame on you, painting you as the 'villain' in the family drama.

Just remember that you are now an adult, and have the right to choose the people that populate your life. Just because you are related to a person does not mean that you have to like them, or that you are obligated to allow them into your life.

You are definitely not obligated to put up with their abuse or mistreatment. Once you set your boundaries, stick to them.

If you need to go full 'no contact' to live your best life, then do so. It's your life and you deserve the best one that you can create. If it means breaking up with your parent or parents, then so be it. Self-preservation must come first.

The narcissistic parent is never going to change. Your relationship is not going to improve. All you can do is accept it for what it is and deal with it.

A Final Wrap-up

1. They may not be a bad person for everyone, but they are for you.

Not all toxic people are toxic to everyone around them. Your toxic mother may do wonderful work at church (where she gets constant praise for her 'selfless' acts) but she cannot and will not ever accept the fact that you are doing something other than following in her footsteps. She constantly berates you for the hours you work, and the people that you are friends with, and every call ends in her hanging up on you - no matter how hard you try to keep the conversation light and happy. You can't be who or what she wants and never will, and she never lets you forget it. You want to curl up in a fetal ball after every call and a visit home takes weeks out of your life to recover.

As hard as it is to face, we have to give ourselves enough to give enough space to live, and more importantly, to thrive. Whether it means limiting your exposure to these toxic encounters, or cutting these people out of your life entirely, you have to make your personal well-being a priority.

It may mean spending less time with someone, putting geographical distance between you,

or removing yourself - temporarily or permanently - from the situation, you have the right to

create a safe and healthy haven for yourself.

2. Understanding that toxic behavior may not be openly aggressive behavior.

Never underestimate the cleverness of the truly toxic person. It's rare that a toxic parent will

show their nasty side in public - the public facade is frequently very congenial, making it that

much more difficult to get people to believe your assertions of abuse. Emotional blackmail is

a favorite tool of their passive aggressive, and can take on many forms, from excluding you in

the conversations at family gatherings (making you feel ostracized) to subtle slights in the

form of dismissive gestures or facial expressions when you are talking.

Although these tactics are subtle, the effect is not, and often leaves you feeling insecure and

unsure about your own thoughts and opinions.

This type of passive aggressive behavior is just as damaging long term to your self-esteem

as the more open verbal abuse. You don't need to put up with it.

3. Toxic people are bullies.

Today, schoolyard bullies are in the news but the truth is, often times the biggest bullies are

in our homes. Wherever you encounter the bully, bullying is never OK. No one has the

someone the right to verbally, emotionally or physically assault another person.

If your bully is your parent or other family member, it's important that you stand up for yourself. Don't give them power over you. It may take a great deal of courage to stand up to your enemies, but it will take even more to stand up to your family.

4. Stop pretending that their behavior is ok. It is not.

We've all been there: done something that we did not want to do because it was simply easier to agree. Or kept your mouth shut while your parent berated you because you just did not want to get into another argument.

Dealing with toxic behavior is exhausting. It wears you down and you find yourself simply being run over again and again because you have simply run out of steam. It simply takes too much energy to defend yourself.

If this is the case, stop. This is simply allowing the toxic behavior to continue, and the effect long term can be disastrous for you.

The short-term peace and quiet afforded by agreeing with the toxic person is just that: short term. They will no doubt cook up another drama and the cycle will just start all over again.

Stand up for yourself. Refuse to participate in the drama and negativity by walking away and putting yourself first for a change.

5. If the toxic behavior turns physical, seek help. Immediately!

There is never a time where physical abuse is ok. Seek help from law enforcement if possible, but whatever the case, remove yourself from the situation immediately. Go to a neighbor, call the police, move to a shelter.

If someone is physically abusive, they are breaking the law and they need to deal with the consequences of their actions and you need to protect yourself. Again - put your own well-being first.

6. Seriously, it's all about them. Not you.

- It's them, not you. KNOW this. Toxic family members will likely try to imply that somehow you've done something wrong. And because the 'feeling guilty' button is quite large on many of us, even the implication that we might have done something wrong can hurt our confidence and unsettle our resolve. Don't let this happen to you. Remember, there is a huge amount of freedom that comes to you when you take nothing personally. Most toxic people behave negatively not just to you, but to everyone they interact with. Even when the situation seems personal - even if you feel directly insulted - it usually has nothing to do with you. What they say and do, and the opinions they have, are based entirely on their own self-reflection.

8. Hating only hurts you.

There is quote that has been attributed to many people, but it rings so true here: 'Hate is too good of an emotion to waste on people you really don't like'.

Hate is an insidious and dark emotion with enormous power. The problem is that when you hate someone, you are giving all of that power to the other person, not to yourself. It takes so much energy to hate someone - is it really worth the effort to hate someone you don't like??

Seek your revenge by living well instead - so much better to prove them wrong and enjoy yourself by living a great life instead.

9. Yes, people can change but only if they want to.

If you are simply dealing with a 'bad' situation, an argument, harsh words & hurt feelings, things can probably be patched up, even if this is a recurring

situation. Some people are simply grumpy and difficult, but with effort they can become more cognizant of their effect on those around them.

Toxic people, especially narcissists, rarely care enough about others to want to change their own behavior. They are the star in their drama, not you, so why should they change.

Just remember, it takes 2 people that want to make a positive change in a relationship for it to happen.

10. Letting go, for good.

No matter what your family may think or say - this is your life. You cannot control toxic family members, all you can do is control your reaction to their actions.

As an entrepreneur, you have probably worked with clients that made your life miserable. Chances are, you removed them from your life.

When dealing with a truly toxic family situation, there may come a time when you are left with no choice but to simply walk away. Put distance between yourself and the toxic family member so that you can heal.

It's not a decision made easily or rashly, but sometimes we have no other choice.

It won't be easy, but it may be necessary if you want to live a normal and healthy life, one of your own choosing.

You may never be able to control all the things toxic family members do to you, but you can decide how it affects you. You have the right to choose who you want beside in your life, and who you choose to call family. The family we choose to keep in our life is not always the same family that the Universe gave us at birth.

It's your life. Life it as you want but above all - have a great one.